Story Prompts
Comedy

The Art of Writing Funny Stories

Created by Mark El-Ayat

For permission requests, write to the publisher, addressed "Attention: Permissions Coordinator," at the address below:

Mark El-Ayat Publishing
Email: Admin@markelayat.com
Website: Markelayat.com

Publisher logo:

Book cover by Mark El-Ayat

First Edition

ISBN: 979-8-9889467-4-8

Printed in United States of America

Year of Publication: 2024

Introduction

Welcome to *Story Prompts Comedy - The Art of Writing Funny Stories*, your gateway into the heart of comedy writing. The following pages will take you on a journey that is not only intended to make you laugh, but also discusses the depth and range of comedy as it is used in storytelling. Whether you're a beginner comedian or an experienced writer seeking to add more humor to your writing, this book is tailored to suit your needs.

The power of comedy lies in its ability to bring people together, going beyond limitations and revealing the absurdities of our existence. This genre requires both clever humor and a compassionate understanding of the human experience. Here, we dive into the craft of creating stories that make readers laugh, think, and feel all at once.

This book offers a collection of prompts across a spectrum of comedic subgenres, from slapstick to satire, each designed to spark your imagination and challenge your storytelling skills. We also provide tools such as plot outlines and character development sheets to help you build your stories with intention and depth. These tools are your scaffolding, supporting you as you construct narratives that are as structurally sound as they are engaging.

Through exploring various subgenres, you'll discover the extent of comedy writing, learning to weave humor through tales of romance, adventure, mystery, and even horror. Consider the prompts as gateways, inviting you to explore uncharted territories of your creative mind.

As you turn each page, remember that comedy is a reflection of life, its joys, its sorrows, and, most importantly, its ridiculousness. Writing funny stories is about finding humor in the unexpected and delight in the mundane.

So, grab your pen, open your mind, and let your heart be light. The world needs more laughter, and it's writers like you who will bring it to life. Welcome to the adventure of writing funny stories.

Let's begin.

Plot Outlines

To write a comedy story, creativity is key. Before diving into each prompt, you'll find a Plot Outline template and a Character Development sheet designed to structure your comedic narrative. When outlining your story, aim for clarity and brevity, using the Notes section for fleshing out details and brainstorming humorous elements.

Plot Outlines serve as the scaffolding of your comedy, providing a structured yet flexible approach to bringing together humor, conflict, and resolution. This ensures your narrative unfolds purposefully, filled with laughter and comedic depth.

Within these pages, you'll discover a framework tailored for any comedic tale. The Plot Outline segments walk you through the important parts of your story, from the funny beginning to the exciting ending.

The Plot Outlines section is your launchpad to dream up, plan, and execute a story that not only entertains but also connects with readers on a humorous level. This is an invitation to thoughtfully plan the path of your story, providing a complete strategy for creating your comedy.

Comedy writing in this case employs the effective classic 3-act structure, which is known for its ability to deliver coherent and captivating narratives that work perfectly with comedic timing. It provides a simple framework, breaking the story into the setup, confrontation, and resolution, facilitating the development of both plot and characters within a comedic context.

The skillful use of this structure effectively increases comedic tension and timing, which are vital elements in the comedy genre, creating a captivating experience for the audience with laughter, unexpected twists, and fulfilling resolutions. By offering a clear framework along with room for imaginative exploration, it becomes the perfect base for diverse comedic stories.

Utilizing this structure ensures that the comedic arc is coherent and impactful, striking a chord with audiences' love for humor and relatable experiences.

Character Development

Character development is crucial in crafting a comedy that resonates and entertains. It's through these carefully sculpted characters that your story comes to life, pulling readers into a universe where every misstep, every line of dialogue, and every absurd situation is pivotal. The sheets included in this workbook are designed to help you delve into the nuances of your main characters' personalities, from their wildest dreams to their most embarrassing blunders, their oddball tendencies to their core values. These investigations will not only reveal how your characters navigate through a maze of comedic trials but will also infuse your narrative with authenticity and laughter.

Remember, the most captivating characters are those that feel genuine and connect with the audience. They are imperfect, they evolve, and they consistently deliver surprises. By deeply examining their development from the outset, you lay the groundwork for a comedy that delights and endures.

In the realm of comedy writing, the complexity and appeal of your characters can transform a straightforward humorous setup into a memorable, laughter-filled adventure.

In comedy writing, characters are crucial for delivering humor. This Character Development Sheet helps you create characters that resonate with readers and excel in comedic situations.

Basic Information: Start with the essentials like name, age, occupation, and appearance to introduce your characters.

Backstory: Explore your characters' histories to find comedic gold. Use their pasts to shape their quirks and comedic potential. A well-crafted backstory not only adds depth but also offers opportunities for humorous revelations and situations.

Personality Traits: Identify key traits that make your characters funny. Are they naive, witty, or overly optimistic? Use these traits to fuel humor in their reactions and interactions.

Goals and Motivations: What do your characters want? Their desires can lead to funny scenarios and pursuits, especially when their goals clash with their realities. Understanding your characters' desires can enhance the excitement and entertainment value of the story.

Fears and Flaws: Comedy thrives on characters' imperfections. Highlight their fears and flaws to create relatable and humorous situations.

Relationship Dynamics: How characters relate to each other is a rich source of comedy. Use their relationships to generate humor through banter, misunderstandings, or unexpected alliances.

Character Arc: Characters should grow or change, even in comedy. Plan their journey from start to finish, ensuring their evolution is both humorous and meaningful.

Dialogue Styles: Develop unique ways each character speaks. Distinct dialogue styles can make conversations funnier and more memorable.

The Character Development sheet is designed to help you create characters that are not only funny but fully realized. By giving careful thought to these elements, you can populate your stories with characters that readers will find funny, cheer for, and remember long after they finish reading.

Your journey begins here.

The Subgenres

Slapstick 1

Farce 13

Satire 25

Parody 37

Romantic Comedy (Rom-Com) 49

Screwball Comedy 61

Black Comedy (Dark Comedy) 73

Observational Comedy 85

Deadpan (Dry Humor) 97

Blue Comedy 109

Slapstick

Slapstick comedy is a genre that revels in exaggerated physical humor and visual gags. This is where you'll find hilarious bloopers and moments that'll crack you up. Rooted in the physical comedy traditions of vaudeville and silent film, slapstick relies on action rather than dialogue to deliver its humor. Its essence lies in the absurdity and extremity of physical situations that characters find themselves in, often leading to chaotic yet hilarious outcomes.

Key Elements:

- <u>Physical Comedy and Exaggeration</u>: The hallmark of slapstick, where humor arises from exaggerated physical movements, expressions, and situations that are deliberately beyond the bounds of normal activity.

- <u>Visual Gags</u>: Slapstick thrives on sight gags, funny costumes, and props that contribute to the comedic effect without the need for words.

- <u>Timing and Pace</u>: The effectiveness of slapstick often depends on precise timing and a fast pace, creating a rhythm that enhances the humor of the physical antics.

Notable Works and Authors:

1. *Three Men in a Boat* by Jerome K. Jerome: A humorous account of three friends and a dog as they embark on a boating holiday on the Thames, filled with comedic misadventures and whimsical digressions.

2. *The Hitchhiker's Guide to the Galaxy* by Douglas Adams: This science fiction comedy follows the intergalactic misadventures of an unwitting human and his alien friend, marked by absurd situations and satirical commentary on life, the universe, and everything.

3. *Good Omens* by Neil Gaiman and Terry Pratchett: A witty tale of an angel and a demon teaming up to prevent the Apocalypse, featuring a series of comedic mishaps, misunderstandings, and attempts to navigate the complexities of human existence.

4. *The Importance of Being Earnest* by Oscar Wilde: A classic play that satirizes Victorian norms and manners, known for its clever wordplay, mistaken identities, and physical comedy, all revolving around the pursuit of love and the importance of being 'earnest.'

Writing Tips:

- **Emphasize the Unexpected:** Build up to your comedic moments in a way that the audience doesn't see coming. The surprise element often makes the physical comedy more impactful.

- **Use Descriptive Language:** Even though slapstick is visual, in writing, you'll need to use vivid descriptions to bring the physical humor to life for your readers.

- **Balance With Story:** Ensure that the slapstick comedy serves the story and character development, rather than overwhelming the narrative.

Plot Outline Template

Title: _____

Setting: _____

Theme: _____

Act 1: Setup

• Introduction to Characters: _____

• Inciting Incident: _____

• Establishing Stakes: _____

Key Elements:

• Establish the type of humor

• Initial humorous conflict

Act 2: The Confrontation

• Deepening Complications: _____

• Midpoint: _____

• Build-Up to Crisis: _____

Key Elements:

• How does the humor evolve or escalate

• The introduction of secondary conflicts or subplots

Act 3: The Resolution

• Climax: _____

• Falling Action: _____

• Denouement/Conclusion: _____

Key Elements:

• Ensure all comedic conflicts are resolved. Stay consistent with the humor

• Highlight how characters have changed

Character Development Sheet

Character Names: _____ / _____

• Nicknames: _____ / _____

• Ages: _____ / _____

• Occupations: _____ / _____

• Physical Descriptions: _____ / _____

• Distinguishing Features (e.g., scars, tattoos):

_____ / _____

Backstory

• Family Background: _____ / _____

• Education & Career Path: _____ / _____

• Significant Past Events: _____ / _____

• Socioeconomic Status: _____ / _____

Personality

• Dominant Traits: _____ / _____

• Fears: _____ / _____

• Desires: _____ / _____

• Hobbies/Interests: _____ / _____

• Habits (good and bad): _____ / _____

• Values & Beliefs: _____ / _____

Relationships

• Current Family Dynamics: _____ / _____

• Friendships: _____ / _____

• Past Romantic Relationships: _____

Goals

• Personal Aspirations: _____ / _____

• Professional Ambitions: _____ / _____

• Romantic Desires: _____ / _____

Conflict

• Internal Conflicts (psychological struggles, fears, uncertainties):

_____

_____

• External Conflicts (with other characters, society, environment):

_____

_____

Character Arc

• Beginning State (personality, situation at the story's start):

_____

_____

• Growth Points (key moments of change):

_____

_____

• End State (transformation or realization by the end):

_____

_____

Dialogue Style

• Speech Patterns (formal, casual, idiosyncratic phrases):

_____ / _____

• Voice (how the character's personality is reflected in dialogue):

_____ / _____

Notes

The Prompt

A character's attempt at a simple task spirals into a hilarious chain of exaggerated mishaps. Describe the scene, focusing on the visual humor and the character's reactions to each escalating absurdity.

Farce

Farce is a comedy that delights in the ridiculousness of its situations. It is known for its unlikely events, cases of mistaken identity, and a fast-paced narrative that keeps the audience laughing throughout. Its foundation is built upon outrageous scenarios and characters who inhabit a world where laughter is prioritized over rationality. What makes farce captivating is its aptitude for pushing the boundaries of believability, establishing a realm where the more absurd the circumstances, the more entertaining it becomes.

Key Elements:

- Improbable Situations: The core of farce is its reliance on highly improbable, often outrageous situations that stack up, creating a domino effect of comedy.

- Mistaken Identities and Misunderstandings: Farce frequently employs mistaken identities, misunderstandings, and deceptions as mechanisms to complicate the plot and heighten the humor.

- Rapid Pacing and Timing: Essential to farce, the rapid pacing keeps the audience on their toes, with timing that precision-targets the delivery of jokes and comedic situations.

Notable Works and Authors:

1. *The Comedy of Errors* by William Shakespeare: A fast-paced farce that doubles the fun with two sets of twins unknowingly crossing paths, leading to mistaken identities, wrongful arrests, and a series of misunderstandings in a single, chaotic day.

2. *Noises Off* by Michael Frayn: A play within a play that takes a behind-the-scenes look at a theatrical production gone awry, showcasing the offstage shenanigans of actors and crew as they fumble through missed cues, love triangles, and on-stage disasters.

3. *Charley's Aunt* by Brandon Thomas: A classic farce involving a pair of Oxford undergraduates who persuade their friend to impersonate Charley's wealthy aunt, leading to a series of humorous deceptions, romantic proposals, and unexpected arrivals.

4. *Lend Me a Tenor* by Ken Ludwig: Set in the 1930s, this comedy unfolds with the mishaps of a world-famous tenor supposed to perform in Cleveland, only to be mistakenly believed dead, prompting a series of impersonations, mistaken identities, and romantic confusions in a luxury hotel suite.

Writing Tips:

- **Keep the Action Moving:** Ensure your plot keeps accelerating, with each new complication more absurd than the last, to maintain the frantic energy that farce requires.

- **Play With Expectations:** Use audience expectations to your advantage, setting them up for one outcome and then delivering another in a way that maximizes comedic effect.

- **Balance Complexity:** While farce thrives on complex situations, ensure your story remains followable, with clear stakes and character motivations amid the chaos.

Plot Outline Template

Title: _____

Setting: _____

Theme: _____

Act 1: Setup

• Introduction to Characters: _____

• Inciting Incident: _____

• Establishing Stakes: _____

Key Elements:

• Establish the type of humor

• Initial humorous conflict

Act 2: The Confrontation

• Deepening Complications: _____

• Midpoint: _____

• Build-Up to Crisis: _____

Key Elements:

• How does the humor evolve or escalate

• The introduction of secondary conflicts or subplots

Act 3: The Resolution

• Climax: _____

• Falling Action: _____

• Denouement/Conclusion: _____

Key Elements:

• Ensure all comedic conflicts are resolved. Stay consistent with the humor

• Highlight how characters have changed

Character Development Sheet

Character Names: _____ / _____

• Nicknames: _____ / _____

• Ages: _____ / _____

• Occupations: _____ / _____

• Physical Descriptions: _____ / _____

• Distinguishing Features (e.g., scars, tattoos):

_____ / _____

Backstory

• Family Background: _____ / _____

• Education & Career Path: _____ / _____

• Significant Past Events: _____ / _____

• Socioeconomic Status: _____ / _____

Personality

• Dominant Traits: _____ / _____

• Fears: _____ / _____

• Desires: _____ / _____

• Hobbies/Interests: _____ / _____

• Habits (good and bad): _____ / _____

• Values & Beliefs: _____ / _____

Relationships

• Current Family Dynamics: _____ / _____

• Friendships: _____ / _____

• Past Romantic Relationships: _____

Goals

• Personal Aspirations: _____ / _____

• Professional Ambitions: _____ / _____

• Romantic Desires: _____ / _____

Conflict

• Internal Conflicts (psychological struggles, fears, uncertainties):

_____

_____

• External Conflicts (with other characters, society, environment):

_____

_____

Character Arc

• Beginning State (personality, situation at the story's start):

_____

_____

• Growth Points (key moments of change):

_____

_____

• End State (transformation or realization by the end):

_____

_____

Dialogue Style

• Speech Patterns (formal, casual, idiosyncratic phrases):

_____ / _____

• Voice (how the character's personality is reflected in dialogue):

_____ / _____

Notes

The Prompt

Two volunteers at a charity auction mistakenly swap a valuable artifact for a fake, sparking a series of comedic mishaps. How do they fix it before the auction ends?

Satire

Satire is all about making fun of society, politics, and human behavior, using wit, irony, and exaggeration to highlight their foolishness. Satire sets itself apart from other comedic genres by not only entertaining but also delivering a message and offering perceptive critiques on real-world problems. It challenges readers to think critically about the subjects it mocks, making it a powerful tool for social and political commentary.

Key Elements:

- Social Critique: The backbone of satire is its critique of societal norms, political systems, human nature, or cultural phenomena, aiming to highlight flaws and prompt change or reflection.

- Irony and Exaggeration: Satire relies heavily on irony and exaggeration to make its point, presenting reality in a distorted mirror that amplifies its absurdities.

- Wit and Humor: While satire aims to critique, it does so through clever humor and sharp wit, engaging readers by making them laugh even as it provokes thought.

Notable Works and Authors:

1. *Gulliver's Travels* by Jonathan Swift: A satirical adventure that critiques human nature and society through the voyages of Lemuel Gulliver to fantastical lands, exposing the follies and vices of the people he encounters and reflecting on the absurdities of the human condition.

2. *Animal Farm* by George Orwell: A powerful satire on totalitarianism and political corruption, Orwell's novella uses a farm of talking animals who overthrow their human farmer to establish their own government, only to replicate the very injustices they sought to escape.

3. *Candide* by Voltaire: A biting satire of optimism and the philosophical ideas of the Enlightenment, following the naive protagonist Candide through a series of increasingly disastrous misadventures around the world, humorously critiquing society, religion, and human folly.

4. *Catch-22* by Joseph Heller: Set during World War II, Heller's novel is a satirical indictment of military bureaucracy and the absurdity of war, centering on a bombardier who is caught in a catch-22: he's considered insane if he willingly continues to fly dangerous missions, but sane if he requests to be relieved from duty, which he cannot be because it's considered a rational act.

Writing Tips:

- **Know Your Target:** Understand deeply the subject you're satirizing. Satire is most effective when it's clear and informed, based on a solid grasp of the topic at hand.

- **Balance Humor and Message:** Find the right balance between making your readers laugh and delivering your critique. Too much of one can dilute the other, weakening the satire.

- **Subtlety Is Key:** Often, satire is most powerful when it's subtle. Rely on the intelligence of your readers to understand and uncover the layers of meaning behind your humor.

Plot Outline Template

Title: _____

Setting: _____

Theme: _____

Act 1: Setup

• Introduction to Characters: _____

• Inciting Incident: _____

• Establishing Stakes: _____

Key Elements:

• Establish the type of humor

• Initial humorous conflict

Act 2: The Confrontation

• Deepening Complications: _____

• Midpoint: _____

• Build-Up to Crisis: _____

Key Elements:

• How does the humor evolve or escalate

• The introduction of secondary conflicts or subplots

Act 3: The Resolution

• Climax: _____

• Falling Action: _____

• Denouement/Conclusion: _____

Key Elements:

• Ensure all comedic conflicts are resolved. Stay consistent with the humor

• Highlight how characters have changed

Character Development Sheet

Character Names: _____ / _____

• Nicknames: _____ / _____

• Ages: _____ / _____

• Occupations: _____ / _____

• Physical Descriptions: _____ / _____

• Distinguishing Features (e.g., scars, tattoos):

_____ / _____

Backstory

• Family Background: _____ / _____

• Education & Career Path: _____ / _____

• Significant Past Events: _____ / _____

• Socioeconomic Status: _____ / _____

Personality

• Dominant Traits: _____ / _____

• Fears: _____ / _____

• Desires: _____ / _____

• Hobbies/Interests: _____ / _____

• Habits (good and bad): _____ / _____

• Values & Beliefs: _____ / _____

Relationships

• Current Family Dynamics: _____ / _____

• Friendships: _____ / _____

• Past Romantic Relationships: _____

Goals

• Personal Aspirations: _____ / _____

• Professional Ambitions: _____ / _____

• Romantic Desires: _____ / _____

Conflict

• Internal Conflicts (psychological struggles, fears, uncertainties):

_____

_____

• External Conflicts (with other characters, society, environment):

_____

_____

Character Arc

• Beginning State (personality, situation at the story's start):

_____

_____

• Growth Points (key moments of change):

_____

_____

• End State (transformation or realization by the end):

_____

_____

Dialogue Style

• Speech Patterns (formal, casual, idiosyncratic phrases):

_____ / _____

• Voice (how the character's personality is reflected in dialogue):

_____ / _____

Notes

The Prompt

In a political mix-up, a satirical manifesto is mistakenly published as government policy, surprisingly winning the public's heart. Describe the policy and the unfolding events.

Parody

Parody is a form of comedy that playfully mocks and amplifies the defining traits, style, or themes of a specific genre, piece of work, or artist. A successful parody requires a delicate balance: it must honor the original source material while simultaneously poking fun at its most recognizable features. This genre thrives on the audience's familiarity with what is being parodied, creating a shared space of humor and appreciation.

Key Elements:

- <u>Imitation with Exaggeration:</u> Central to parody is the imitation of the source material, but with significant exaggeration to highlight its quirks, faults, or clichés in a humorous light.

- <u>Familiarity with the Source:</u> The effectiveness of parody often depends on the audience's familiarity with the original work. The more recognizable the source, the more likely the parody will resonate.

- <u>Humorous Critique:</u> While parody aims to amuse, it often also carries a subtle critique of the original work or genre, commenting on its conventions, predictability, or any perceived lack of depth.

Notable Works and Authors:

1. *Don Quixote* by Miguel de Cervantes: This timeless work parodies the popular chivalric romances of Cervantes' era, following the misadventures of Don Quixote, who, driven mad by reading too many such romances, sets out to revive knighthood and bring justice to the world, often with hilariously misguided outcomes.

2. *Bored of the Rings* by Harvard Lampoon: A humorous take on Tolkien's epic fantasy, this parody reimagines the quest to destroy the One Ring with sharp wit and irreverence, substituting Middle-earth with "Middle Earth" and its characters with amusing counterparts, making for a hilariously twisted journey.

3. *Pride and Prejudice and Zombies* by Seth Grahame-Smith: This novel melds the refined social mores of Jane Austen's classic with the undead horror of zombie fiction, creating an alternate Regency England where Elizabeth Bennet and her sisters not only navigate the complexities of love and society but also slay zombies.

4. *The Wind Done Gone* by Alice Randall: A retelling of "Gone with the Wind" from the perspective of Cynara, a slave on Scarlett O'Hara's plantation, this parody critiques and subverts the original's romanticized view of the South, offering a fresh and provocative take on the story and its characters.

Writing Tips:

- **Deep Knowledge of the Source:** To effectively parody something, you must understand it well. This knowledge allows you to identify and exaggerate the most ripe aspects for humor.

- **Respectful Ridicule:** Aim to poke fun without malice. The best parodies come from a place of respect and affection for the source material.

- **Creativity in Exaggeration:** Use your creative license to push boundaries and explore how far you can stretch the recognizable elements of the source while still keeping the parody recognizable.

Plot Outline Template

Title: _____

Setting: _____

Theme: _____

Act 1: Setup

• Introduction to Characters: _____

• Inciting Incident: _____

• Establishing Stakes: _____

Key Elements:

• Establish the type of humor

• Initial humorous conflict

Act 2: The Confrontation

• Deepening Complications: _____

• Midpoint: _____

• Build-Up to Crisis: _____

Key Elements:

• How does the humor evolve or escalate

• The introduction of secondary conflicts or subplots

Act 3: The Resolution

• Climax: _____

• Falling Action: _____

• Denouement/Conclusion: _____

Key Elements:

• Ensure all comedic conflicts are resolved. Stay consistent with the humor

• Highlight how characters have changed

Character Development Sheet

Character Names: _____ / _____

• Nicknames: _____ / _____

• Ages: _____ / _____

• Occupations: _____ / _____

• Physical Descriptions: _____ / _____

• Distinguishing Features (e.g., scars, tattoos):

_____ / _____

Backstory

• Family Background: _____ / _____

• Education & Career Path: _____ / _____

• Significant Past Events: _____ / _____

• Socioeconomic Status: _____ / _____

Personality

• Dominant Traits: _____ / _____

• Fears: _____ / _____

• Desires: _____ / _____

• Hobbies/Interests: _____ / _____

• Habits (good and bad): _____ / _____

• Values & Beliefs: _____ / _____

Relationships

• Current Family Dynamics: _____ / _____

• Friendships: _____ / _____

• Past Romantic Relationships: _____

Goals

• Personal Aspirations: _____ / _____

• Professional Ambitions: _____ / _____

• Romantic Desires: _____ / _____

Conflict

• Internal Conflicts (psychological struggles, fears, uncertainties):

_____

_____

• External Conflicts (with other characters, society, environment):

_____

_____

Character Arc

• Beginning State (personality, situation at the story's start):

_____

_____

• Growth Points (key moments of change):

_____

_____

• End State (transformation or realization by the end):

_____

_____

Dialogue Style

• Speech Patterns (formal, casual, idiosyncratic phrases):

_____ / _____

• Voice (how the character's personality is reflected in dialogue):

_____ / _____

Notes

The Prompt

Choose a well-known story, genre, or author. Imagine an alternative version where key elements are exaggerated to comic effect. How do the characters, setting, or plot change?

Romantic Comedy

Romantic Comedy combines the sweetness of romance with the light-heartedness of humor, creating stories that explore the complexities of love through amusing situations and witty dialogue. In this genre, characters go on a journey through relationships, dealing with funny obstacles and misunderstandings. What makes romantic comedies so charming is their ability to make us laugh and cheer for love to conquer all, providing a delightful ending that satisfies our hearts and sense of humor.

Key Elements:

- **Chemistry and Conflict:** The heart to a rom-com is the chemistry between the main characters. They have funny conflicts, misunderstandings, or weird situations that bring them closer or drive them apart.

- **Humorous Obstacles:** Romantic comedy characters often encounter funny obstacles like mistaken identity, unfortunate events, or interference from friends and family.

- **Happy or Hopeful Endings:** While the journey may be filled with comedic turmoil, romantic comedies typically conclude with a resolution that brings the characters together, reaffirming the power of love coupled with laughter.

Notable Works and Authors:

1. *Bridget Jones's Diary* by Helen Fielding: Follows Bridget Jones, a single woman in London, as she humorously documents her quest for love, personal growth, and the perfect balance in life through her diary entries.

2. *Pride and Prejudice* by Jane Austen: Centers on Elizabeth Bennet and her four sisters as they navigate love, societal expectations, and personal pride, especially when Elizabeth encounters the enigmatic Mr. Darcy.

3. *To All the Boys I've Loved Before* by Jenny Han: Lara Jean's secret love letters to her past crushes are mysteriously mailed, leading to a series of heartwarming yet awkward situations that redefine her approach to love and relationships.

4. *Crazy Rich Asians* by Kevin Kwan: Rachel Chu finds herself immersed in the extravagant world of Singapore's elite after discovering her boyfriend, Nicholas Young, hails from one of Asia's wealthiest families, sparking a journey filled with opulence, drama, and humor.

Writing Tips:

- **Focus on Character Development:** Develop well-rounded characters whose quirks, flaws, and growth are central to both the humor and the romance of your story.

- **Balance Humor with Heart:** While the comedy drives the plot, ensure there's enough emotional depth and genuine connection between characters to make the romance believable and engaging.

- **Play with Tropes:** Use familiar romantic comedy tropes creatively—subvert them, twist them, or play them straight with a fresh perspective to keep the story both comforting and surprising.

Plot Outline Template

Title: _____

Setting: _____

Theme: _____

Act 1: Setup

• Introduction to Characters: _____

• Inciting Incident: _____

• Establishing Stakes: _____

Key Elements:

• Establish the type of humor

• Initial humorous conflict

Act 2: The Confrontation

• Deepening Complications: _____

• Midpoint: _____

• Build-Up to Crisis: _____

Key Elements:

• How does the humor evolve or escalate

• The introduction of secondary conflicts or subplots

Act 3: The Resolution

• Climax: _____

• Falling Action: _____

• Denouement/Conclusion: _____

Key Elements:

• Ensure all comedic conflicts are resolved. Stay consistent with the humor

• Highlight how characters have changed

Character Development Sheet

Character Names: _____ / _____

- Nicknames: _____ / _____

- Ages: _____ / _____

- Occupations: _____ / _____

- Physical Descriptions: _____ / _____

- Distinguishing Features (e.g., scars, tattoos):

  _____ / _____

Backstory

- Family Background: _____ / _____

- Education & Career Path: _____ / _____

- Significant Past Events: _____ / _____

- Socioeconomic Status: _____ / _____

Personality

- Dominant Traits: _____ / _____

- Fears: _____ / _____

- Desires: _____ / _____

- Hobbies/Interests: _____ / _____

- Habits (good and bad): _____ / _____

- Values & Beliefs: _____ / _____

Relationships

- Current Family Dynamics: _____ / _____

- Friendships: _____ / _____

- Past Romantic Relationships: _____

Goals

• Personal Aspirations: _____ / _____

• Professional Ambitions: _____ / _____

• Romantic Desires: _____ / _____

Conflict

• Internal Conflicts (psychological struggles, fears, uncertainties):

_____

_____

• External Conflicts (with other characters, society, environment):

_____

_____

Character Arc

• Beginning State (personality, situation at the story's start):

_____

_____

• Growth Points (key moments of change):

_____

_____

• End State (transformation or realization by the end):

_____

_____

Dialogue Style

• Speech Patterns (formal, casual, idiosyncratic phrases):

_____ / _____

• Voice (how the character's personality is reflected in dialogue):

_____ / _____

Notes

The Prompt

A bookstore owner and a tech entrepreneur share a shop and spar over their views, only to find romance brewing amidst their business rivalry. How do they handle love and competition?

Screwball Comedy

Screwball Comedy is all about fast talking, quirky characters, and crazy situations that result in hilarious misunderstandings and love complications. This genre from the early 20th century is all about defying social norms and expectations. It's all about strong women who outwit or match their male counterparts. Screwball comedy is a fun blend of romance, clever jokes, crazy antics, and poking fun at society.

Key Elements:

- Rapid-Fire Dialogue: Screwball comedy is known for its quick and witty banter that keeps audiences engaged. The dialogue is packed with double meanings, clever retorts, and quick comebacks.

- Romantic Conflict and Chemistry: Screwball comedies thrive on romantic conflicts caused by misunderstandings, deceptions, or class distinctions, fueling the comedic narrative and highlighting protagonist chemistry.

- Eccentric Characters and Situations: Screwball comedy is all about weird characters in fancy places, with crazy situations that clash with their efforts to act normal.

Notable Works and Authors:

1. *Bringing Up Baby* by Hagar Wilde: A screwball comedy classic where a paleontologist and a heiress embark on a chaotic adventure with a leopard named Baby, leading to romantic mishaps and uproarious situations.

2. *My Man Godfrey* by Eric Hatch: In this Depression-era story, a homeless man becomes a butler for a wealthy, eccentric family, offering a humorous exploration of class differences and zany character antics.

3. *The Princess Bride* by William Goldman: Combines adventure, romance, and humor in a tale of heroism and true love, peppered with witty dialogue and memorable characters in a storybook setting.

4. *Confessions of a Shopaholic* by Sophie Kinsella: Follows Rebecca Bloomwood, a shopping-obsessed journalist, as she navigates through financial and romantic troubles with humor and heart.

5. *Where'd You Go, Bernadette* by Maria Semple: A story about eccentric architect Bernadette Fox's disappearance, as her daughter unravels the mystery with a humorous twist, showcasing a modern take on screwball comedy elements.

Writing Tips:

- **Master the Art of Banter:** Develop your skill in writing quick-witted dialogue that bounces seamlessly between characters, serving as the core interaction that drives both humor and romance.

- **Create Conflict with Stakes:** Ensure that the romantic and situational conflicts are meaningful, with clear stakes that justify the characters' over-the-top actions and decisions.

- **Embrace the Absurd:** Don't shy away from scenarios that push the boundaries of believability. The more outlandish the situation, the more it lends itself to screwball comedy, provided you keep the characters' reactions grounded and relatable.

Plot Outline Template

Title: _____

Setting: _____

Theme: _____

Act 1: Setup

• Introduction to Characters: _____

• Inciting Incident: _____

• Establishing Stakes: _____

Key Elements:

• Establish the type of humor

• Initial humorous conflict

Act 2: The Confrontation

• Deepening Complications: _____

• Midpoint: _____

• Build-Up to Crisis: _____

Key Elements:

• How does the humor evolve or escalate

• The introduction of secondary conflicts or subplots

Act 3: The Resolution

• Climax: _____

• Falling Action: _____

• Denouement/Conclusion: _____

Key Elements:

• Ensure all comedic conflicts are resolved. Stay consistent with the humor

• Highlight how characters have changed

Character Development Sheet

Character Names: _____ / _____

• Nicknames: _____ / _____

• Ages: _____ / _____

• Occupations: _____ / _____

• Physical Descriptions: _____ / _____

• Distinguishing Features (e.g., scars, tattoos):

_____ / _____

Backstory

• Family Background: _____ / _____

• Education & Career Path: _____ / _____

• Significant Past Events: _____ / _____

• Socioeconomic Status: _____ / _____

Personality

• Dominant Traits: _____ / _____

• Fears: _____ / _____

• Desires: _____ / _____

• Hobbies/Interests: _____ / _____

• Habits (good and bad): _____ / _____

• Values & Beliefs: _____ / _____

Relationships

• Current Family Dynamics: _____ / _____

• Friendships: _____ / _____

• Past Romantic Relationships: _____

Goals

• Personal Aspirations: _____ / _____

• Professional Ambitions: _____ / _____

• Romantic Desires: _____ / _____

Conflict

• Internal Conflicts (psychological struggles, fears, uncertainties):

_____

_____

• External Conflicts (with other characters, society, environment):

_____

_____

Character Arc

• Beginning State (personality, situation at the story's start):

_____

_____

• Growth Points (key moments of change):

_____

_____

• End State (transformation or realization by the end):

_____

_____

Dialogue Style

• Speech Patterns (formal, casual, idiosyncratic phrases):

_____ / _____

• Voice (how the character's personality is reflected in dialogue):

_____ / _____

Notes

The Prompt

A demanding event planner and a carefree chef face off while setting up a lavish wedding, navigating their clash and bizarre couple requests. Can they make it work?

Black Comedy

Black Comedy, also known as Dark Comedy, explores subjects and scenarios that are typically seen as serious, taboo, or morbid, but approaches them with humor and satire. It requires a delicate balance, as it seeks to entertain while making poignant observations about life's more grim aspects, often leading to a cathartic experience for both the writer and the reader.

Key Elements:

- Morbidity with Wit: The cornerstone of black comedy is its ability to approach grim or taboo subjects with a clever, often irreverent wit, making light of situations that are typically off-limits for humor.

- Satirical Perspective: Many black comedies offer a satirical take on their dark themes, critiquing societal norms, human behavior, or institutions through their humorous portrayal of otherwise serious subjects.

- Complex Emotional Layers: This subgenre often evokes a complex mix of emotions, from amusement to discomfort, forcing readers to confront their feelings about the darker sides of life and humanity.

Notable Works and Authors:

1. *Slaughterhouse-Five* by Kurt Vonnegut: A darkly humorous take on war and existence, following Billy Pilgrim's surreal time-traveling journey through the absurdities of life and the destruction of war.

2. *American Psycho* by Bret Easton Ellis: Satirizes 1980s consumerism and excess through the life of Patrick Bateman, a serial killer hiding behind a facade of corporate success.

3. *The Metamorphosis* by Franz Kafka: Explores alienation and indifference with dark humor, telling the story of Gregor Samsa's transformation into an insect and his family's reaction.

4. *A Confederacy of Dunces* by John Kennedy Toole: Centers on Ignatius J. Reilly's comedic misadventures in New Orleans, offering a satirical critique of society through a cast of eccentric characters.

Writing Tips:

- **Find Humor in the Darkness:** Look for the inherent absurdity in dark situations or themes. The contrast between the subject matter and the humor can be strikingly effective.

- **Maintain Empathy:** While exploring dark themes, it's important to handle sensitive topics with a degree of empathy and understanding, ensuring that the humor enhances rather than detracts from the narrative.

- **Use Satire and Irony:** Employ satire and irony to deepen the comedic effect and to provide commentary on the darker aspects of the story, enriching the narrative with layers of meaning.

Plot Outline Template

Title: _____

Setting: _____

Theme: _____

Act 1: Setup

• Introduction to Characters: _____

• Inciting Incident: _____

• Establishing Stakes: _____

Key Elements:

• Establish the type of humor

• Initial humorous conflict

Act 2: The Confrontation

• Deepening Complications: _____

• Midpoint: _____

• Build-Up to Crisis: _____

Key Elements:

• How does the humor evolve or escalate

• The introduction of secondary conflicts or subplots

Act 3: The Resolution

• Climax: _____

• Falling Action: _____

• Denouement/Conclusion: _____

Key Elements:

• Ensure all comedic conflicts are resolved. Stay consistent with the humor

• Highlight how characters have changed

Character Development Sheet

Character Names: _____ / _____

• Nicknames: _____ / _____

• Ages: _____ / _____

• Occupations: _____ / _____

• Physical Descriptions: _____ / _____

• Distinguishing Features (e.g., scars, tattoos):

_____ / _____

Backstory

• Family Background: _____ / _____

• Education & Career Path: _____ / _____

• Significant Past Events: _____ / _____

• Socioeconomic Status: _____ / _____

Personality

• Dominant Traits: _____ / _____

• Fears: _____ / _____

• Desires: _____ / _____

• Hobbies/Interests: _____ / _____

• Habits (good and bad): _____ / _____

• Values & Beliefs: _____ / _____

Relationships

• Current Family Dynamics: _____ / _____

• Friendships: _____ / _____

• Past Romantic Relationships: _____

Goals

• Personal Aspirations: _____ / _____

• Professional Ambitions: _____ / _____

• Romantic Desires: _____ / _____

Conflict

• Internal Conflicts (psychological struggles, fears, uncertainties):

_____

_____

• External Conflicts (with other characters, society, environment):

_____

_____

Character Arc

• Beginning State (personality, situation at the story's start):

_____

_____

• Growth Points (key moments of change):

_____

_____

• End State (transformation or realization by the end):

_____

_____

Dialogue Style

• Speech Patterns (formal, casual, idiosyncratic phrases):

_____ / _____

• Voice (how the character's personality is reflected in dialogue):

_____ / _____

Notes

The Prompt

A corporate executive leads a double life as a vigilante by night, targeting unethical colleagues in absurdly over-the-top ways. As his actions spiral, how does he juggle his dark hobby with boardroom politics?

Observational Comedy

Observational Comedy shines a light on the everyday, turning the mundane aspects of daily life into sources of humor and insight. This subgenre is characterized by its relatable content, as comedians and writers draw from common experiences, social norms, and the quirks of human behavior that often go unnoticed. It hits home because it speaks to what we all go through, with a funny twist on life's crazy moments.

Key Elements:

- Relatable Experiences: The foundation of observational comedy is its focus on everyday situations and experiences that audiences instantly recognize and connect with, such as dating, family dynamics, work life, and social interactions.

- Sharp Insight and Commentary: Beyond simply noting everyday occurrences, it often includes a layer of commentary, offering sharp insights into why these common experiences are humorous or absurd.

- Subtle Exaggeration: While much observational comedy is rooted in truth, a slight exaggeration of circumstances or behaviors can amplify the humor, making the ordinary extraordinary.

Notable Works and Authors:

Me Talk Pretty One Day by David Sedaris: Sedaris turns his keen eye and sharp wit on his own life experiences, from learning French to teaching a writing workshop, transforming the mundane into moments of absurdity and insight.

Bossypants by Tina Fey: Fey recounts her journey from a nerdy kid to a comedy icon, infusing stories from her personal and professional life with her trademark humor, tackling everything from feminism to the craziness of show business.

SeinLanguage by Jerry Seinfeld: Seinfeld offers his observations on daily life, from the trivialities of eating cereal to the social complexities of dating, capturing the essence of his comedic genius in print.

Is Everyone Hanging Out Without Me? (And Other Concerns) by Mindy Kaling: Kaling shares her thoughts and experiences on a variety of topics with humor and heart, from Hollywood's beauty standards to the awkwardness of growing up.

Dress Your Family in Corduroy and Denim by David Sedaris: Sedaris dives into stories of his quirky family and upbringing, finding universal humor in the peculiarities of his life and relationships.

Writing Tips:

- **Focus on the Familiar:** Start with personal experiences or common situations, and explore the humor in those relatable moments.

- **Refine Your Perspective:** Observational comedy thrives on unique perspectives. Work on finding an original angle or insight on everyday occurrences that sets your commentary apart.

- **Practice Restraint:** The power of observational comedy often lies in its subtlety. Practice restraint in your writing, allowing the humor to emerge naturally from the situations and your reflections on them.

Plot Outline Template

Title: _____

Setting: _____

Theme: _____

Act 1: Setup

• Introduction to Characters: _____

• Inciting Incident: _____

• Establishing Stakes: _____

Key Elements:

• Establish the type of humor

• Initial humorous conflict

Act 2: The Confrontation

• Deepening Complications: _____

• Midpoint: _____

• Build-Up to Crisis: _____

Key Elements:

• How does the humor evolve or escalate

• The introduction of secondary conflicts or subplots

Act 3: The Resolution

• Climax: _____

• Falling Action: _____

• Denouement/Conclusion: _____

Key Elements:

• Ensure all comedic conflicts are resolved. Stay consistent with the humor

• Highlight how characters have changed

Character Development Sheet

Character Names: _____ / _____

• Nicknames: _____ / _____

• Ages: _____ / _____

• Occupations: _____ / _____

• Physical Descriptions: _____ / _____

• Distinguishing Features (e.g., scars, tattoos):

_____ / _____

Backstory

• Family Background: _____ / _____

• Education & Career Path: _____ / _____

• Significant Past Events: _____ / _____

• Socioeconomic Status: _____ / _____

Personality

• Dominant Traits: _____ / _____

• Fears: _____ / _____

• Desires: _____ / _____

• Hobbies/Interests: _____ / _____

• Habits (good and bad): _____ / _____

• Values & Beliefs: _____ / _____

Relationships

• Current Family Dynamics: _____ / _____

• Friendships: _____ / _____

• Past Romantic Relationships: _____

Goals

- Personal Aspirations: _____ / _____

- Professional Ambitions: _____ / _____

- Romantic Desires: _____ / _____

Conflict

- Internal Conflicts (psychological struggles, fears, uncertainties):

_____

_____

- External Conflicts (with other characters, society, environment):

_____

_____

Character Arc

- Beginning State (personality, situation at the story's start):

_____

_____

- Growth Points (key moments of change):

_____

_____

- End State (transformation or realization by the end):

_____

_____

Dialogue Style

- Speech Patterns (formal, casual, idiosyncratic phrases):

_____ / _____

- Voice (how the character's personality is reflected in dialogue):

_____ / _____

Notes

The Prompt

Craft a funny story based on a real family gathering you've been to, emphasizing the peculiar family members and unforeseen incidents.

Deadpan

Deadpan, or dry humor, is characterized by its understated and unemotional delivery, where the comedy comes from the contrast between the expressionless presentation and the wit of the content itself. This subgenre thrives on subtlety, often requiring the audience to pay close attention to catch the humor embedded in seemingly straightforward statements or situations. The strength of deadpan humor lies in its ability to surprise and engage the audience, making them work a little to uncover the joke, which often revolves around absurdity, irony, or a stark observation made with a straight face.

Key Elements:

- Understated Delivery: Deadpan humor is characterized by its stoic and emotionless presentation, allowing the audience to focus on the subtle humor in the content.

- Intelligent Wit: Deadpan humor relies on clever wordplay and unexpected observations for laughter.

- Subtle Absurdity and Irony: This style is presented in a matter-of-fact manner that heightens the comedic effect by juxtaposing the ordinary with the nonsensical.

Notable Works and Authors:

1. *Catcher in the Rye* by J.D. Salinger: Chronicles the experiences of Holden Caulfield, a disenchanted teenager wandering New York City, delivering his cynical observations with Salinger's trademark deadpan humor.

2. *A Man Called Ove* by Fredrik Backman: Follows the life of Ove, a curmudgeonly old man whose attempts to end his life are continually thwarted by his neighbors' needs. The novel balances dark themes with a deadpan humor that celebrates life's absurdities.

3. *Less* by Andrew Sean Greer: Follows Arthur Less, a failed novelist on the brink of turning fifty, who embarks on a worldwide adventure to avoid the wedding of his former lover. Greer infuses the narrative with a gentle deadpan humor as Less navigates ridiculous and poignant situations alike.

4. *Rosencrantz and Guildenstern Are Dead* by Tom Stoppard: This play turns Shakespeare's "Hamlet" on its head, focusing on two minor characters, Rosencrantz and Guildenstern. Stoppard's clever use of deadpan dialogue and existential humor examines the larger questions of fate and free will.

Writing Tips:

- **Master the Art of Restraint:** In writing deadpan humor, less is often more. Practice restraint in your delivery, allowing the humor to emerge through subtle cues and intelligent wordplay rather than overt jokes.

- **Focus on Contrast:** Enhance your deadpan humor by creating contrast between what is said and what is meant, or between the ordinariness of the delivery and the unexpectedness of the content.

- **Cultivate a Unique Voice:** Deadpan humor often relies on the narrator's or character's unique perspective. Develop a distinct narrative voice that can deliver dry observations with a straight face.

Plot Outline Template

Title: _____

Setting: _____

Theme: _____

Act 1: Setup

• Introduction to Characters: _____

• Inciting Incident: _____

• Establishing Stakes: _____

Key Elements:

• Establish the type of humor

• Initial humorous conflict

Act 2: The Confrontation

• Deepening Complications: _____

• Midpoint: _____

• Build-Up to Crisis: _____

Key Elements:

• How does the humor evolve or escalate

• The introduction of secondary conflicts or subplots

Act 3: The Resolution

• Climax: _____

• Falling Action: _____

• Denouement/Conclusion: _____

Key Elements:

• Ensure all comedic conflicts are resolved. Stay consistent with the humor

• Highlight how characters have changed

Character Development Sheet

Character Names: _____ / _____

• Nicknames: _____ / _____

• Ages: _____ / _____

• Occupations: _____ / _____

• Physical Descriptions: _____ / _____

• Distinguishing Features (e.g., scars, tattoos):

_____ / _____

Backstory

• Family Background: _____ / _____

• Education & Career Path: _____ / _____

• Significant Past Events: _____ / _____

• Socioeconomic Status: _____ / _____

Personality

• Dominant Traits: _____ / _____

• Fears: _____ / _____

• Desires: _____ / _____

• Hobbies/Interests: _____ / _____

• Habits (good and bad): _____ / _____

• Values & Beliefs: _____ / _____

Relationships

• Current Family Dynamics: _____ / _____

• Friendships: _____ / _____

• Past Romantic Relationships: _____

Goals

• Personal Aspirations: _____ / _____

• Professional Ambitions: _____ / _____

• Romantic Desires: _____ / _____

Conflict

• Internal Conflicts (psychological struggles, fears, uncertainties):

_____

_____

• External Conflicts (with other characters, society, environment):

_____

_____

Character Arc

• Beginning State (personality, situation at the story's start):

_____

_____

• Growth Points (key moments of change):

_____

_____

• End State (transformation or realization by the end):

_____

_____

Dialogue Style

• Speech Patterns (formal, casual, idiosyncratic phrases):

_____ / _____

• Voice (how the character's personality is reflected in dialogue):

_____ / _____

Notes

The Prompt

Craft a scene where a character faces an absurd or ironic situation but reacts (or narrates) with complete emotional detachment.

Blue Comedy

Blue Comedy delves into themes and content that are adult-oriented, often exploring topics like sexuality, profanity, and other taboo subjects with a humorous lens. It relies on the shock value and the candidness of its material to elicit laughter, making it both provocative and immensely relatable to adult audiences.

Key Elements:

- <u>Adult Themes and Language:</u> Central to blue comedy is its focus on adult themes, including sexual content, using explicit language and imagery that might be deemed offensive or too graphic for more conservative comedy genres.

- <u>Candidness and Shock Value:</u> This style often capitalizes on the shock value of its content, presenting taboo subjects candidly and without euphemism, challenging societal norms and expectations about what is "acceptable" humor.

- <u>Relatability and Honesty:</u> Despite its edginess, the strength of blue comedy lies in its honesty and the universal relatability of its themes. It speaks to the shared, often unspoken experiences of adulthood, creating a space for laughter and release.

Notable Works and Authors:

1. *Fear and Loathing in Las Vegas* by Hunter S. Thompson: Thompson's infamous chronicle of a trip to Las Vegas under the influence of a plethora of drugs serves as a savage critique of the American Dream, peppered with raucous humor and a candid look at the counterculture of the 1960s.

Chelsea Chelsea Bang Bang by Chelsea Handler: Handler's collection of essays offers a no-holds-barred look into her life, with candid discussions on sex, dating, and the quirks of everyday life, all delivered with her signature sharp, blue humor.

I Hope They Serve Beer in Hell by Tucker Max: Max's memoir recounts his adventures (or misadventures) in excessive drinking, casual sex, and general debauchery, pushing the boundaries of social acceptability with crude humor and unapologetic frankness.

Choke by Chuck Palahniuk: The story of Victor Mancini, a medical school dropout with a sex addiction, who concocts an elaborate scheme to pay for his mother's care in a nursing home. Palahniuk brings together dark comedy with themes of addiction, dysfunctional relationships, and the search for personal identity in a disillusioned society.

Writing Tips:

- **Know Your Audience:** Blue comedy isn't for everyone. Be mindful of your audience and the platforms you're using to share your work, ensuring it's appropriate for those who will be reading it.

- **Balance Humor with Substance:** While the shock value can be appealing, the best blue comedy also offers depth and insight into the human condition, providing more than just laughs.

- **Use Explicit Content Judiciously:** While blue comedy involves adult themes, the use of explicit content should serve the humor and the story, rather than being gratuitous or offensive for the sake of shock alone.

Plot Outline Template

Title: _____

Setting: _____

Theme: _____

Act 1: Setup

• Introduction to Characters: _____

• Inciting Incident: _____

• Establishing Stakes: _____

Key Elements:

• Establish the type of humor

• Initial humorous conflict

Act 2: The Confrontation

• Deepening Complications: _____

• Midpoint: _____

• Build-Up to Crisis: _____

Key Elements:

• How does the humor evolve or escalate

• The introduction of secondary conflicts or subplots

Act 3: The Resolution

• Climax: _____

• Falling Action: _____

• Denouement/Conclusion: _____

Key Elements:

• Ensure all comedic conflicts are resolved. Stay consistent with the humor

• Highlight how characters have changed

Character Development Sheet

Character Names: _____ / _____

• Nicknames: _____ / _____

• Ages: _____ / _____

• Occupations: _____ / _____

• Physical Descriptions: _____ / _____

• Distinguishing Features (e.g., scars, tattoos):

_____ / _____

Backstory

• Family Background: _____ / _____

• Education & Career Path: _____ / _____

• Significant Past Events: _____ / _____

• Socioeconomic Status: _____ / _____

Personality

• Dominant Traits: _____ / _____

• Fears: _____ / _____

• Desires: _____ / _____

• Hobbies/Interests: _____ / _____

• Habits (good and bad): _____ / _____

• Values & Beliefs: _____ / _____

Relationships

• Current Family Dynamics: _____ / _____

• Friendships: _____ / _____

• Past Romantic Relationships: _____

Goals

• Personal Aspirations: _____ / _____

• Professional Ambitions: _____ / _____

• Romantic Desires: _____ / _____

Conflict

• Internal Conflicts (psychological struggles, fears, uncertainties):

_____

_____

• External Conflicts (with other characters, society, environment):

_____

_____

Character Arc

• Beginning State (personality, situation at the story's start):

_____

_____

• Growth Points (key moments of change):

_____

_____

• End State (transformation or realization by the end):

_____

_____

Dialogue Style

• Speech Patterns (formal, casual, idiosyncratic phrases):

_____ / _____

• Voice (how the character's personality is reflected in dialogue):

_____ / _____

Notes

The Prompt

A comedian finds a diary filled with the scandalous and hilarious secrets of a small town's residents and turns it into comedy material, causing uproar. What happens next?

Thank You!

As we reach the end of our journey together through these prompts, I hope you've found sparks of inspiration, moments of challenge, and above all, a deeper love for the art of storytelling. If this book has played a part in your writing journey, I invite you to share your experience by leaving a review.

Your insights not only celebrate our shared passion for storytelling but also guide fellow writers to resources that could enlighten their own creative paths. Whether it's a brief note or an in-depth reflection, your feedback is a beacon for the community and a treasure for me.

Thank you for embracing the adventure of writing with me. Your engagement and support illuminate the way forward.

With warmest regards,

Mark El-Ayat

STORY PROMPTS

This book is one in a series that features various genres of story prompts. Take your creative journey to the next level with our Story Prompts books. They're designed to inspire and guide your storytelling across various genres.

Find new worlds, interesting characters, and exciting plots that are waiting for your unique voice.

Our Story Prompts series is here to help writers at any stage, with a wide range of prompts to dive into different themes, characters, and plots. Don't stop writing! Your next amazing story starts right here!

For more information and to discover other books in the series, visit my website www.markelayat.com